MW00928555

DATE: ....

THIS JOURNAL BELONGS TO

....

....

....

....

Made in the USA
Monee, IL
22 December 2021

86856766R00072